TALES RETOLD

POEMS

Marcelle Kasprowicz

De Lodis Publishing
ISBN: 0-9776047-4-8

OTHER PUBLICATIONS
by author

Organza Skies: Poems from the Davis Mountains, 2007
Children Playing with Leopards, 2012
Out of Light Darkness, 2013
Her Blue Touch, 2014

ACKNOWLEDGEMENTS

Eat a Peach, "When the Plague"
Goblin Fruit, "Lion in Love"
Di-verse-city 1999,"Rumpelstiltskin"
De Lodis Publishing 2007, Organza Skies:Poems from the Davis Mountains, "The Fisherman and the Crescent Moon","The Miser and the Moon"

DEDICATION

For all those who once were children

TALES RETOLD

TABLE OF CONTENTS

Rumpelstiltskin

Come to me
I'll make your ewes lamb, your mares foal
I'll make your meadows green, your wheat fields gold
but when darkness rolls in, when the wind whines
tugging at your shutters, lapping at your front door
hold on to your sons, hold on to your daughters
I'll come for your first born if you don't know my name

Come to me
I'll spare no sweat for you, I'll work night and day
I'll spin all your straw into gold
but when darkness rolls in, when the wind growls
nipping at your shutters, gnawing at your front door
hold on to your sons, hold on to your daughters
I'll come for your first born if you don't know my name

Come to me

I'll give you youth forever lasting
I'll give you love forever pleasing
but when darkness rolls in, when the wind howls
tearing at your shutters, forcing down your door
hold on to your sons, hold on to your daughters
I'll come for your first born if you don't know my name

And if you come looking for me tonight
I'll be roasting tender meats on my campfire
I'll be mum, I'll do my jig in darkness
You won't notice the curl in my crimson slippers
nor the name burnished on my chest
I'll keep my waistcoat buttoned tight

Tonight
hold your sons and daughters tight
I'm coming for your first born
and you don't know my name

The Fateful Dozen

Was it written in the spiraling heat
of freshly chopped chicken livers
or Mrs. Z's dog-eared tarot cards?
Who's to say?

Why should a dozen be twelve
rather than thirteen?
Therein, I'm convinced
lies the root of the evil to come

***

In a kingdom
where life went on forever
a new princess was born
about to be christened

From keep to moat

the castle
was a merry caldron
boiling over
spilling into the streets
where children romped
rattling wooden spoons
dipping from every pot
where dogs, tongues out
for young bloods' sweet drippings
haunted the roasting spits

In the cavernous hall
young maids all in a row
sat at the long table
polishing silverware
twelve in all
—silverware, that's a known fact,
comes in just twelve settings—
In the candlelight
their dimpled cheeks glowed
and rose like leavened bread
twelve cherubs
blowing the annunciation

in their trumpets

***

How could anyone have known?
Only twelve honored guests
were expected
And then Death made her entrance
brandishing her silver spinning wheel
like a sword

Who to turn to?
The extended-hour-super-store
had not yet arrived
An old tin setting was hastily polished
but the die was cast

Oh, the princess would live
for a while
until one day
Well, you know
the spinning wheel...
Unless of course
the right prince came along

The Giant of Lilliput

The dark giant of Lilliput is laid out
but his core is on fire
He's been run through
with a roasting spit
At each end
a thousand little men turn
turn
turn
A thousand more run around
with little golden pots
to collect the drippings and baste
baste
baste
A thousand more
tip-toe through the burning ashes
and stoke the flame

When they stop

a gaggle of sparks

hisses, spits at the smoldering ashes

and shoots up in the cold sky

All night

they fall

one by one

ice kisses

seething on Earth's giant back

The dark giant of Lilliput

is on fire

He's been run through

with a roasting spit

At each end

a thousand little men will burn

burn

burn

Gingerbread Man

Gingerbread, Gingerbread, Gingerbread man
Who loves you, Gingerbread man?

Who loves your pudgy puckered thighs
Who loves your fat little neck
Who loves you to the tip of your sweet button nose?
Mommy and Daddy
Gingerbread man

It was the day of the Lord
and times were hard
They scraped the bottom of their flour bin
added the last of their brown sugar
and together, they made you
turned the oven on low

set it for nine minutes (or was it nine months?)

and sat down to wait

to build castles in the air

Would you turn out golden brown

like the wheat fields you came from?

Would you take on brown sugar's darker hue?

Would they eat you right out of the oven

mouth-scalding hot?

Would they wait?

How long could they wait?

Meanwhile they missed all the action

Yes, you, in the oven

flexing your muscles

doing calisthenics

getting ready for opening time

And when it came

you hopped right out and took off running
with Mommy and Daddy in hot pursuit

Times were hard
You did not find comfort along the way
only a gauntlet of spades and pitchforks
and rows of teeth clacking
like nutcrackers closing on empty

Times were hard, about to get harder
A lazy river
coming from lord knows where
meandered right across your path
cutting off your escape

Your condition does not allow for skinny-dipping
so what could you do but take up the offer
of that gorgeous and generous stranger
who proposed a dry ride across

on the sumptuous velvet of his red fur?

You hopped right into his mouth

and it didn't clap on empty!

If only times hadn't been so hard

If only the river hadn't meandered across your path

If only gorgeous and generous were wed

You might still be running today!

Gingerbread, Gingerbread, Gingerbread man

Who loves you, Gingerbread man?

Little Red Riding Hood

GRANDMOTHER:

Someone locked me up
in this dark cupboard
Day and night I stumble
feeling around for my wicker basket
my little red riding hood

Take me home
to your bright cupboard
I'll be a mouse
I want only
the crumbs of your life
Take me home

GRANDAUGHTER:

Grandma Grandma
your cupboard is bare
Your little red riding hood
the one you wore

over those Shirley Temple curls
over those suckling babe's arms
over the blue pearls
of those china doll eyes
where did you stash it?
* * *

Is that you in the woods
setting your wicker basket
down on the grass
playing hopscotch with him
on the sandy path?
You're teasing him now
tickling his whiskers
pulling on his tail
cheating honestly
making fun of that big old tongue
lolling out drooling red
over your good-enough-to-eat cheeks
slapping those clumsy paws
tugging at your ribbons

And now you made him mad

the old satyr
and there he goes running off ahead
his ugly tail between his legs

Here you are happy as a lark
with a throatful of singing-games
skipping along
all the way to the cottage
barely tall enough
to tip back that heavy latch

And there he is in bed
a black mountain
under her lacy night bonnet
and your china doll eyes
they're popping out
as big as a bullfrog's
on a summer night pond

And you are saying
Oh Grandma
What big teeth you have...
He rears up

tears off bonnet and flannel gown
his bristles so many knives
He tastes your dimples already
But you're a red flash
on those little tap-dancing shoes
and his belly too heavy still

Oh Grandma
I see no woodcutter
no kindly ax
Only you, someone transformed by time
soon to be dispersed

Oh, Grandma Grandma
What shall I do? Quick
the ribbons on my hood
my ribbons
like yours
are coming undone

The Ugly Duckling

Oh little duckling
egg of my nest
down of my breast
flesh of my tomorrows
your twenty-one days are up
Out in the barnyard
your brothers and sisters
are already playing
I hear their dear little quacks
Hurry up and join them

Eleven perfect eggs
blue-green like I was
—my mother told me so—
You couldn't tell one from the other
And they all hatched on the very same
sunny spring day
And then there's you
just a little too big

just a little too white
Still, I hear the same little clock ticking
and yes, I even see your egg-tooth now
I know you will be big and beautiful
You took so long!
You will be the envy of all the barnyard
and your mommy will love you

Ah, so much time, so much effort
for you?
Where is that sunkissed down
the plump little boat of flesh
I was expecting
how can you be so scrawny?
People will think I haven't been a good mother
Ah, little one
will your brothers know you?
Will they love you?

Out there in the barnyard
things are tough enough
even for those who belong
Watch out for the chickens on the high ridge

near their chicken house
They think they're better than we are
They never give us a break
Look at those uppity hens
counting their henpecked broods
watch how they groom
those ugly little crests on their head
You'd think they belong to an ivy league school
Do you know they always look down on our kind
just because we live pond-side
and like to get down and wallow in the mud?
Little do they know
they'll still end up on the master's table

Ah, but now, you
Where will you fit?
You don't look like us
You don't look like them

Ah, little hatchling
will your brothers know you
will your mother love you?

The Goose That Laid the Golden Eggs

Talk about luck

Winning at lotto couldn't compare

They owned a goose

a goose that laid golden eggs

She laid them matter-of-factly

wherever she happened to be

in meadow grasses silvered by morning dews

in damp mosses under trees

in the dry comfort of her dusty straw nest

plopped them down she did in the mud and steamy refuse

amidst the hustle and bustle of the barnyard floor

Such a lackadaisical attitude

toward a most valuable commodity

raised concerns amongst her handlers

They met around a goose-grease smeared kitchen table

Those who had never laid an egg

golden or otherwise

put forth it was immoral

to degrade such miracles

on the filth of a barnyard floor

"Secure and regulate" they argued

"Confine the goose to a vault tidy and sterile

Keep her under twenty-four hour watch"

Others cackled that the sight of the divine fowl

should be shared with all

They proposed an altar of sorts

where the anointed bird could display her powers

to an awed and generous audience

A few who in their youth

had recklessly taken watches apart

and been sorry for it

tearfully pleaded for the status quo

while the somewhat schooled sustained

that blood and guts alone

could not be at the root of such wealth and beauty

but rather a sublimely intricate mechanism

worth discovering and duplicating

Tempers flared

cackles rose

feathers flew

Matters were fortuitously resolved

as they sometimes are

when a famished uniformed entity

commandeered the unfortunate fowl

and twisted the discord's innocent neck

When the goose was cut open

it was found to be full of goose

Lion In Love

based on Le Lion Amoureux by La Fontaine

In days of yore
when people and animals consorted still
lived a lion so smitten with a lady
he asked for her hand in marriage

To her father he went
with his mane duly slicked back
—almost tamed—
lowered his lordly stare
dropped one knee to the hard cobblestone
and half fumbled his request

The lord of the castle
quaking in his seven-league boots
acquiesced
What could he do?
One swat of that terrible paw

and he would be minced meat
They brought in the lady
shy as a dove on the outside
hard as nails on the inside
She sized up her prospects
and was duly impressed
—almost in love—
Lion melted at her feet
They were wed

Sweet husband, she cooed
before their honeymoon
behold my fair neck
I fear you will draw blood
when we embrace
Please let me trim your lordly nails
just a little
Lion looked at her fair neck
and deep into her eyes
He acquiesced
What could he do?
He was in love

Quick, she ran down to the garden
borrowed the rosebush clippers
—golden of course—
and pared his nails
left five bleeding nubs on each paw

Furthermore, she cooed
when we kiss
I fear your lordly teeth
will bite my tender lips
Please let me file them
just a little
Lion looked at the nubs on his paws
and deep into her eyes
He sighed and acquiesced
What could he do?

Quick, she ran down to the stables
borrowed the horse-shoeing file
—golden of course—
came back and filed away
to the gum

*After that
she did with him as she pleased*

Metamorphosis

Based on " La chatte métamorphosée en femme "
by La Fontaine

Pretty cat
my sweet pet
my fair companion
said the master
would that your perfect teeth
open into a tender smile
Would that your lustrous fur
be locks on my pillow
would that your dainty paws
be hands and return my caress
and that you be my ladylove
my wife

And so it came to pass
and she had dominion over the lord

over the house

No more scraps begged from the master's hand
but whole pheasants now ordered and served
on frail translucent ware
No more naps on the cold cobbled floor
long nights now in warm feather beds
with the master at her feet

No more hunting
What for?

Yet, what was she to think
when in her dreams
mice freshly caught appeared
and squirmed on her porcelain plate?

Oh, what was she to do
when mice still roamed unchecked
in her dark castle halls?

The Little Mermaid

Oh, beware, beware of fairy tales
Beware of transformations

Why tempt fate?
Would you give your sixteen-year-old
the keys to your new car?
They gave this young mermaid
the keys to the kingdom of light
Take a peek above the waves
they said then come back
Didn't they know
you can't keep them down under
once they've seen the moonlit sea?

Well, it happened
She set her brand-new eyes on a prince
and by the pain she felt inside
like knives dressing out her heart
she knew
She was in love

Don't be too hard on her
After all, people have been known
to sell their soul
She traded her tongue for a pair of legs

In her torment she sought advice from Mrs. Z
gypsy of the deep, forked-tongued
with sea snakes around both wrists
She laid her laminated tarot cards
on the red coral table
and gave it to her straight
Your tongue and its golden voice
for a pair of nice long legs
I do the surgery in my office
without anesthesia
after all
good things shouldn't come easy
And there will be some residual pain
Each step you take
will be like walking on knives

She accepted
How could she not?
Worse knives were carving out her heart

Well, it worked
She found herself lying on a moonlit beach
the same handsome prince moon-eyed
gaping at her
She looked into his eyes
He looked into hers
and waited
and waited
for the right words to come
out of her heart-shaped mouth

Alas, she had no voice
As he was rather inexperienced
—dense you might say—
in matters of love
and couldn't even read lips
he never knew
By now the constant pain in her legs

often made her cross, bad company
He soon tired of her
found a more down-to-earth fun-loving companion
and married her

What would you have her do?
She had drowned her fishtail
There was no turning back
and as sure as innocent fish
are harpooned and scaled every day
she was being butchered

Pills were not an option
but castle turrets were
overhanging the sea
One moonlit night
she jumped
and became
foam on the sea
                    Oh, foams on the sea
                    You are my voice
                    Speak for me

The Glass Slipper

Belle of the night
Belle of the ball
Moon has lost
her sparkling glass slipper
and shines her light
along the milky-way
looking for it

The Fisherman and the Crescent Moon

Oh crescent moon
said the fisherman
since I saw the loveliness of your shape
and touched the silk of your trembling skin
on the waves
I love you
Please let me sail up to you
through your balmy waters
and reel you in
There's room in my skiff
for two
I'll lay you down beside me
and you will be forever
my wife

Sweet fisherman
said the moon
since I watched you heave your heavy nets ashore
and tasted the silver salt of your flesh

I've wished it could be so
Yet if you take me from my sky
the shine you love will go
the way of your young maidens' glow
the way of your fishes' sparkle
Sweet fisherman
do you still want me?

Mad with love
the fisherman sailed the skies
reeled in his moon
but when he laid her in his skiff
embraced only a whiff of sparkling silver dust
while around him the winds blew mean
over the pitch-black seas

The Miser and the Moon

The miser bites into the moon

to see if it is real

He spits it back

into the springs

Poor moon

To be treated that way!

The Milkmaid (Updated)

I am running
skipping my way to the store
kicking my heels way up
to my backside
bouncing the blue ball of my dream

On my left shoulder
the red mesh bag
where recyclable yoghurt jars
are clanging
'Green' was a behavior
mandated by scarcity then

I am counting my chickens ...

A pack of spearmint gum
five cents
A chocolate bar
ten cents ...

A misstep
of course
due to a forgivable welling up of emotions

Perhaps
a flaw in reasoning
One tends to underestimate the fragility
of eggshells   glass   dreams

Beauty and the Beast

It happened once upon a time
when castles sprouted
from the fat of the land
when good and evil were knights
at each other's throat
when wild beasts roamed

I was young and beautiful
I lived in my father's house
tended the poisonous garden of my family
with bare hands
Nothing grew there but nettles of envy
Blooms were as brittle as lifeless
as the ones I kept pressed in my diary

Every night I dreamed of a rose
a rose as big as alive
as a doe's beating heart
and when I reached out and touched it

from its thorns
dripped petals of blood

On the dark side of the land
past the hungry forest of wolves
farther than my white mare would go
lived a fearful beast
all hair teeth and nails
He hunted along the banks
of his secret marshes
among the trembling reeds
or stalked his game
across the fallow fields of his kingdom
With the thorns of his nails
he could tear any young doe's heart out
yet every night
when he looked at himself
in the brooding mirror of his marshes
it was his face
he tore out in shame and anger

On the sheltered side of his castle
he lovingly tended

a hidden rose garden
and with his fearful nails
awkwardly tilled the earth
barely dared to lift his eyes
up to the blooms

You heard of my father's mistake
his lost wealth
and his fateful promise

Ah, better to die a quick death
and save someone you love!

I rode away unnoticed
Snow's white panther
followed us
filled in our tracks
with her padded feet
smothered silence
Sleep was overtaking me
I looked at my white mare
her flanks dripped with blood
and under her

a rose laid in the snow

Like an icy squall
the castle rose
dark
in my face

Ah, you know the rest
The fearsome beast
You know how I tended
the brooding garden of his innocent sins
You know how
from bewitched ground
I delivered a heart
more tender than a doe's heart
more beautiful than a rose

Lorelei

In a city
Built on the banks of a river
There lived a dark enchantress

Her hair was the color of poppy fields
From which she rose one day
And when they breathed her heady powders
Men had taste left only for her
And eyes only for the brazier of her hair
Where their freedom
Burned

To the judge who sentenced him today
On his knees he said
I throw myself on your mercy
Please don't send me away
I can't bear to live
Without the sting
Of her needles of fire

The judge chooses his two best guards
Take this man
Deliver him to the dungeon
High in the mountains
There he will be confined
For his own safety
Until we tear the heart
Out of his insanity

The path is steep
Under the moonlight
The guards stumble
And he hears the sound of her voice
She is calling to him
With her ensnaring song
He sees her reflection
Burning in the river
She's waiting for him

Like a deer he bounds
and from the highest rock
he leaps

Wolf and Dog

In times wild
when every kind pulled its weight
when Wolf and Dog
had enough civility left
to converse
before sinking their teeth
in each other's flesh
Wolf spoke

Dog
You have enough teeth
to crush the strongest bones
enough teeth to clasp a throat
and bring down a grown buck

Why allow this weak
devious creature
to keep you chained
to sink steel teeth

into your throat

Wolf
If you only knew

My master
has taught me
the depraved art
of turning teeth
against one's own flesh
and helped me discover
the torment the ecstasy
of one who belongs

Orpheus

It was not his tormenting haste
to see her beloved face

It was not an irresistible itch
that caused Orpheus
to turn around
at the edge of the underworld

It was not a challenge
to the gods
nor a belief
in the overwhelming power
of his music

Think about it
At the last minute
he must have lost his nerve

What right did he have

to pluck her out of her dark cocoon
a cotton-wool half-life

What right did he have
to drag her out
into the deceptive light of this world
knowing a life
is destined to fall
on jagged rocks
and bleed

Penelope Won't Wait

Before you left
I watched you try out your cast-out armor
I could hear its rusty hinges
creaking

My sky was a loom then
In its weft and warp
I caught only flightless birds

You chose war

When it's over
you'll blame the winds
for keeping you away
But how can one seduced by mythical waters
return to unruffled seas

I won't wait for you
I am weaving forbidden birds

---

and soon will set them free

The Pied Piper

You appeared one day at the crook of Main Street
loaded with the coal-black bundle of ages
Yet when you walked
you merely kissed the cobblestones
with the snow of your silent slipper

A stranger strangely remembered

You made no bones about your identity
laid your pied cards flat on the table
But we live on the edge
and play the weasel's game
A deal is a good deal
if you don't have to pay

And now you've taken them all

down to the littlest one

tripping over his night-shirt to keep up

See how they follow you

singing and skipping along

to the bewitching trills of your tune

See how they jump laughing over the edge

See how they endure now

impaled on the steeples of our sins

Temptation

Oh, Frog, said the scorpion
the sands across the water hole are calling me
Please let me climb onto your back
and ferry me to the other side
I'll be gentle, I'll be careful
I'll hold my stinger way up high

Oh, Frog, the crossing is easy
I watch your swimmer's legs propel our little skiff
through the clear iris of your pond's still waters
Already the winds speak to me of hot, welcoming sands
We're almost there

Oh, Frog, the tender jelly of your flesh
ripples naked under my claws
and the burning nettle of your green, liquid skin
seeps under my armor...
We're almost there, we're almost there, but Frog
Oh, forgive me

I am not made of stone

The Ark or, A Giraffe's Reflections

Your pets have disappointed you
so all of us must atone

I have been herded
into this crowded ark
Head and neck above all
I watch the waters rise
struggling bodies
rafting toward their maker

Yet
all of us
lived by the sword you gave us
never strayed

Was it the unique pattern
on my hide
predetermination
dumb luck

I was saved

Next to me
the tigers refuse to watch
They have thrown themselves down
on the planks
paws over ears
They can't stand the cries
They squeeze their eyes closed
attempting to shut out
images of their drowning cubs

This flood
such scouring
and the earth
a prey slaughtered
and left to rot

When the Plague Came to Town

When the plague came to town
gone were her mourning robes
gone her acolytes and their dooming pitch
gone her rats back into her sleeves
gone the fever of her groins
the bursting fruit of her flesh

This time
she brought her jugglers her flags
her brass bands
her flute
her glittering sandman's dust
and when she crooked her finger
like sleepwalkers we all followed

Marcelle Kasprowicz was born in France. She received an M.A. from the University of Texas at Austin. Marcelle writes in English and French. She also translates her French poems in English. Many of her poems have been published in reviews, anthologies and on line. She was awarded several prizes. She has published four books, *Organza Skies: Poems from the Davis Mountains* in 2007, *Children Playing with Leopards* in 2012, *Out of Light Darkness* in 2012, and *Her Blue Touch* in 2014.